DOLLEY MADISON

FIRST LADY

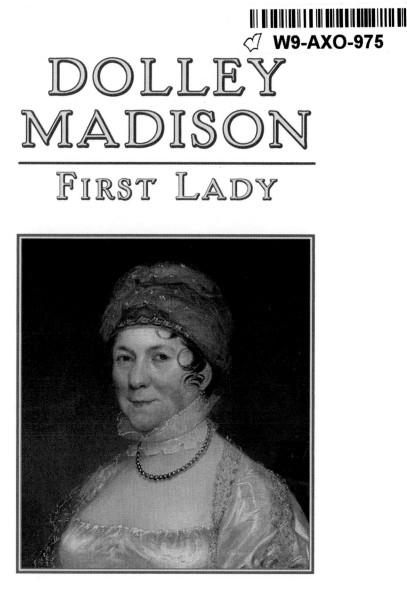

by Bette Beer

HOUGHTON MIFFLIN   BOSTON

Dolley Madison

Dolley Payne was born in North Carolina in 1768. She grew up in Virginia.

James Madison as a young man

Later, Dolley and her family moved to Philadelphia. Dolley met James Madison. They were married in 1794.

The White House in 1814

In 1809 James Madison became President of the United States. The President's wife is called the First Lady. Dolley became the First Lady.

The Red Room

They lived in Washington, D.C.,
in the White House.
Dolley decorated
the White House.
She helped make it
a beautiful place.

Dancing at a party

Dolley wore fancy clothes.
She had dinner parties.
She was very friendly and
made people feel welcome
in her home.

The Federal Room

Many people came to the
White House.
Dolley always remembered
people's names.
She was a great hostess.

British ready for war

In 1814 the United States was at war with Britain. British soldiers marched toward Washington, D.C. President Madison left to be with the United States Army.

British attack

Now Dolley was in charge of
the White House.
The British soldiers were close.
Dolley was afraid that
they would destroy her home.

Dolley saving important papers

Dolley knew she had
to leave the White House.
She wanted to save
some valuable things.
She started to pack them.

Painting saved by Dolley Madison

Dolley took President Madison's important papers.
She saved a painting
of President George Washington.
She even saved red curtains.

The White House after it was burned

When it was safe,
the Madisons came back.
The White House
had been burned.
The Madisons stayed
in another house.
Dolley welcomed people there.

Dolley Madison, First Lady

People thought Dolley
was a hero.
She was very smart.
She was also brave.
Dolley Madison was
an important First Lady.

Montpelier

In 1817 James Madison
was finished being President.
Dolley and James left
Washington, D.C.

The Madisons moved
to a farm in Virginia.
Their farm was called
Montpelier (mahnt PEEL yur).
Dolley welcomed people there.

Dolley Madison was First Lady from 1809 to 1817. Here are some important things she did.

- decorated the White House

- hosted dinners and events

- made visitors feel welcome

- took charge of the White House when the President was gone

- saved valuable things from the White House

- helped the President in many ways